If Life were fair, Horses would ride half the time

The truth about life, by
Ben Goode

Illustrated by
David Mecham

The Truth About Life ™

Published by:
Apricot Press
Box 1611
American Fork, Utah
84003

books @ apricotpress.com
www.apricotpress.com

Copyright 2002 by E. W. Allred.
All rights reserved. No part of this book may be
reproduced or transmitted in any form or by any
means (electronic or mechanical, including
photocopy, recording, or any information retrieval
system) without the written permission of the
publisher.

ISBN 1-885027-17-6

Cover Design & Layout by David Mecham
Printed in the United States of America

Forward

Some of my more perceptive readers will notice right away that many of the chapter titles in this book have little or nothing to do with the actual content of those chapters. From this, you may have concluded that this book is nothing but a big scam to take your money and that the author was probably too dense or unprincipled to make the effort to come up with an entire book filled with stuff exclusively on this topic.

Instead of scam or fraud, we prefer the view that the glass is 1/116 full, and we would like to point out that at least the chapter headings deal specifically with the topic of fairness, and that "fairness" is at least a theme that we come back to periodically. If this bothers you, you can take comfort in the knowledge that you have discovered one more crystal clear example of the principle that life is not fair; in fact, you have one more first hand experience. Maybe this will inspire you to write a book. Have a nice day.

Further Forward

I write for a living…pardon me, I mean I promote for a living, but I have to make time to write some stuff for people to buy when I promote it, so I am constantly in need of good material. Unfortunately, for writers, life is not fair. It seems I always think of my best ideas when there is no pen or paper around; therefore, I am also paranoid. I normally keep 6 or 7 pens hidden on my person or in bodily orifices. In spite of these efforts, I still seem to come up with my best ideas when I'm showering, hang-gliding, or going over Niagara Falls on a leaky water weenie. I guess this also means that for you readers, life isn't fair either, because you have missed all my best ideas and all you have to read is this second-rate drivel. Regardless, don't stop buying my cast-off material. That wouldn't be fair.

Contents

Life
is not fair

"People with no children are always the best parents." - Richard Weinerman

For some reason known only to Him, God made the world unfair. You don't have to be very bright to observe that fairness is not natural in our world. Ugly, ill-tempered animals eat cute, nice ones; smog will kill us, but it produces breathtaking, lovely sunsets; some people are born in Greenland, while perverts get to produce TV shows.

What makes this so confusing is, in order to make life fair for one person, God must make it unfair for someone else. At the same moment a farmer is praying for rain to water his garbanzo beans, his lovely daughter is praying that it will be sunny for her garden wedding; a sea bass is fleeing for his life from a barracuda who will starve to death if he doesn't get something to eat; my office sometimes hides a cell phone in my golf bag so they can find me when I should be back there suffering through another meeting.

Yet, even though life clearly isn't supposed to be fair, we normal people are determined to make it so. We clump into different groups, which promise to make everything fairer for us than it is for the rich people. We elect politicians who promise to suspend the laws of nature. We buy diet products so we will look like the people on the advertisements who have symmetrical eyes, long legs, and clear skin.

Like a herd of lemmings in heat[1] with over-programmed imprinting tendencies on our frontal lobes[2], most of us will follow anybody who promises to make our life more fair just as long as someone else is paying and just as long as it doesn't require any effort on our part. A wise guy I know once observed that if the promoters of fairness were to succeed in

---

[1]Wouldn't that be something if, at this precise moment, our federal government was spending our money to study lemmings in heat. Ponder that. On the other hand, I hope I haven't given any of my mentally unstable scientific readers any crazy ideas.

[2]This assumes that I have some readers who are animal biologists, and I don't mean guys like Rick, who just watch fish swim up the dams on the Columbia either. I could probably tell you more about lemmings than they can.

making life fair, they would be out of some great paying jobs. So, in addition to the laws of nature, we also have this fact to insure that these clowns will never be the ones to make life fair either.

So, if you are feeling picked on, and let's be honest, judging by the decibel level of your whining out there, there must be millions of you, we have an old fashioned remedy: PERSPECTIVE. For the times when you are made extra aware that life isn't fair, here are a bunch of poor creatures who are probably even more wretched than you...at least we hope so.

Creatures toward whom life has probably been even less fair than toward the rest of us

A fish is forced to breathe and live in the same water in which it bathes and in which it discharges...whatever it discharges.

●●●●●●●●●●●●●●●●●●

A snake is unable to scratch where it itches. How fair can that be?

●●●●●●●●●●●●●●●●●●

You could be a mouse and be stuck right near the bottom of the food chain with virtually everything trying to eat you.

Wolves' only friends are environmentalists
and taxidermists. Sad.

● ● ● ● ● ● ● ● ● ● ● ● ● ● ● ● ● ●

A guy praying mantis spends his whole life
trying to hook up with a hot female and when
he finally succeeds, she eats him.

● ● ● ● ● ● ● ● ● ● ● ● ● ● ● ● ● ●

If you were a weasel, through no fault of your
own, you would have a bad reputation and
everyone would be trying to shoot you.

● ● ● ● ● ● ● ● ● ● ● ● ● ● ● ● ● ●

A frog has no hair and therefore suffers
terribly in the snow and cold.

● ● ● ● ● ● ● ● ● ● ● ● ● ● ● ● ● ●

Unless you neuter him, a Billy goat smells
worse than almost anything I can think of.

● ● ● ● ● ● ● ● ● ● ● ● ● ● ● ● ● ●

Swine have eyesight that is so bad they have to
taste everything on the ground to have any idea
what it is, and they are known universally by the
demeaning slur-form of their name.

● ● ● ● ● ● ● ● ● ● ● ● ● ● ● ● ● ●

A fruit fly's entire life cycle is over in 48 hours. What great things could YOU accomplish on that schedule?

●●●●●●●●●●●●●●●●●●

Further evidence that God did not intend for life to be fair

Work, effort, and nasty food are all required if a person is to stay in shape.

●●●●●●●●●●●●●●●●●●

People often show their love for a beloved pet by having it neutered.

●●●●●●●●●●●●●●●●●●

In countries where marriages are arranged, exceptional women often find themselves married to some pretty, how could I say, below average guys.

●●●●●●●●●●●●●●●●●●

The better tasting the food, the more surely it will kill you.

●●●●●●●●●●●●●●●●●●

Younger sisters only get the Nintendo when nobody else wants it.

●●●●●●●●●●●●●●●●●●

5

Howard Stern, Martha Stewart, and Dennis Rodman are (were) rich and famous.

●●●●●●●●●●●●●●●●●

As we get older and older and accumulate more and more wisdom, it gets harder and harder to remember it.

●●●●●●●●●●●●●●●●●

The Middle East.

●●●●●●●●●●●●●●●●●

Years of drought will always end with a downpour on your wedding day.

●●●●●●●●●●●●●●●●●

All hot, trendy fashions further enhance the appearance of people who are already young, fit, attractive, long-legged and sleek, and make the rest of us, who desperately need help, look silly.

●●●●●●●●●●●●●●●●●

Millions of rabid fans probably will never tune in all over the world to watch a math competition.

●●●●●●●●●●●●●●●●●

When you are young and athletic and active, everyone thinks you're smart. Then, when you are older and really ARE smart, nobody wants to listen because they're afraid you will make them feel guilty for doing the stupid things they already made up their minds to do anyway.

••••••••••••••••••••

Frogs never get a turn eating OUR legs.

••••••••••••••••••••

Generally, the worse the job, the lower the pay, and visa-versa.

••••••••••••••••••••

If life were fair, you would get the worst zits you ever grew while on vacation with your parents to Eastern Europe instead of on picture day or for the prom.

••••••••••••••••••••

 Many people
have observed
that often
life is not fair

"Half-a-wit is better than no wit at all."
- Ben Jammin

If life were fair...

If life were fair, men would get menstrual cramps
and labor contractions.

•••••••••••••••••

If life were fair, no one would be both stupid
AND ugly.

If life were fair, cats would have to empty
their own litter boxes.

• • • • • • • • • • • • • • • • • •

If life were fair, stupid drivers would
have to follow themselves.

• • • • • • • • • • • • • • • • • •

If life were fair, half the guys would be attracted
to homely women and visa-versa.

• • • • • • • • • • • • • • • • • •

If life were fair, your best drive wouldn't always
find the only gopher hole on the fairway.

• • • • • • • • • • • • • • • • • •

If life were fair, telemarketers would sometimes
call when you're not sitting down to eat.

• • • • • • • • • • • • • • • • • •

If life were fair, the more honest people were, the
richer they would become.

• • • • • • • • • • • • • • • • • •

If life were fair, bugs would have little helmets
enabling them to shatter the windshield some of
the time.

• • • • • • • • • • • • • • • • • •

If life were fair, kids would appreciate everything their parents do for them, before they became parents themselves.

● ● ● ● ● ● ● ● ● ● ● ● ● ● ● ● ● ●

If life were fair, snakes would either have legs or wings.

● ● ● ● ● ● ● ● ● ● ● ● ● ● ● ● ●

If life were fair, good-tasting food would be good for you.

● ● ● ● ● ● ● ● ● ● ● ● ● ● ● ● ●

If life were fair, your gold fish would get to go out often.

● ● ● ● ● ● ● ● ● ● ● ● ● ● ● ● ●

If life were fair, your good days would be as good as your bad ones are bad, and you would have an equal number of each.

● ● ● ● ● ● ● ● ● ● ● ● ● ● ● ● ●

If life were fair, your jam sandwich would sometimes land face up.

● ● ● ● ● ● ● ● ● ● ● ● ● ● ● ● ●

If life were fair, dogs would have their turn making the fleas itch.

If life were fair, annoying celebrities would
struggle to earn minimum wage.

● ● ● ● ● ● ● ● ● ● ● ● ● ● ● ● ● ●

If life were fair, people would be exactly as stupid
or as smart as they look.

● ● ● ● ● ● ● ● ● ● ● ● ● ● ● ● ● ●

If life were fair, politicians would work for a
living and spend their own money.

● ● ● ● ● ● ● ● ● ● ● ● ● ● ● ● ● ●

If life were fair, baby birds could jump
back into the nest.

● ● ● ● ● ● ● ● ● ● ● ● ● ● ● ● ● ●

If life were fair, no one would hear the stupid
things you say.

● ● ● ● ● ● ● ● ● ● ● ● ● ● ● ● ● ●

If life were fair, drunk drivers would only kill
themselves.

● ● ● ● ● ● ● ● ● ● ● ● ● ● ● ● ● ●

If life were fair, everyone would have a turn
winning the lottery.

● ● ● ● ● ● ● ● ● ● ● ● ● ● ● ● ● ●

If life were fair, athlete's foot would be
known as politicians' mouth.

● ● ● ● ● ● ● ● ● ● ● ● ● ● ● ● ●

If life were fair, whenever people lie their noses
would grow.

● ● ● ● ● ● ● ● ● ● ● ● ● ● ● ● ●

If life were fair, a grasshopper versus a duck
would be a fair fight.

● ● ● ● ● ● ● ● ● ● ● ● ● ● ● ● ●

If life were fair, pets would get to neuter their
owners some of the time.

● ● ● ● ● ● ● ● ● ● ● ● ● ● ● ● ●

If life were fair, occasionally I would win a
sweepstakes, drawing, lottery, or something.

● ● ● ● ● ● ● ● ● ● ● ● ● ● ● ● ●

If life were fair, Fifi would have to actually do
something productive or go hungry.

● ● ● ● ● ● ● ● ● ● ● ● ● ● ● ● ●

If life were fair, the meaner you are, the uglier
you would be.

● ● ● ● ● ● ● ● ● ● ● ● ● ● ● ● ●

If life were fair, these therapies would work

If life were fair, "Putting-your-hands-over-your-ears-therapy" should cure bad news.

●●●●●●●●●●●●●●●●●●

"Ice cream and chocolate therapy" would cure obesity.

●●●●●●●●●●●●●●●●●●

"Convoluted excuse therapy" would make it better whenever you do something you wish you hadn't.

●●●●●●●●●●●●●●●●●●

If life were fair, good therapy for belligerent and disobedient teens should be lecture therapy done to a background of 60's music.

●●●●●●●●●●●●●●●●●●

If life were fair, "elevating-the-decibel-level-of-your-voice-therapy" would cure stupidity.

●●●●●●●●●●●●●●●●●●

Excessive credit card debt could usually be cured by "public lottery therapy".

Fatigue could be cured by pizza.

● ● ● ● ● ● ● ● ● ● ● ● ● ● ● ● ● ●

If life were fair, Arthritis would be cured by a
good nap.

● ● ● ● ● ● ● ● ● ● ● ● ● ● ● ● ● ●

Mr. Clean would work on
dirty politicians.

● ● ● ● ● ● ● ● ● ● ● ● ● ● ● ● ● ●

If life were fair, strength and endurance could be
improved with Twinkie therapy.

● ● ● ● ● ● ● ● ● ● ● ● ● ● ● ● ● ●

Acne would be cured by
video games therapy.

● ● ● ● ● ● ● ● ● ● ● ● ● ● ● ● ● ●

If life were fair, "shaky-resolve-therapy" would
cure substance abuse.

● ● ● ● ● ● ● ● ● ● ● ● ● ● ● ● ● ●

Banging your head against the wall would cure
stress, and really bad stress could be cured by
banging someone else's head against the wall.

● ● ● ● ● ● ● ● ● ● ● ● ● ● ● ● ● ●

Dyslexia could be cured by looking at
things cross-eyed.

If life were fair, practicing law could be cured
by going to church.

● ● ● ● ● ● ● ● ● ● ● ● ● ● ● ● ● ● ●

Heart disease would be cured by
"pudding, French fries, and
beef jerky therapy."

● ● ● ● ● ● ● ● ● ● ● ● ● ● ● ● ● ● ●

"More-government-programs therapy" would
cure sky rocketing medical costs.

● ● ● ● ● ● ● ● ● ● ● ● ● ● ● ● ● ● ●

"Making-the-other-guy's-nose-bleed-therapy"
would cure nosebleeds.

● ● ● ● ● ● ● ● ● ● ● ● ● ● ● ● ● ● ●

If life were fair,"Biting sarcasm therapy" would
make someone love you.

● ● ● ● ● ● ● ● ● ● ● ● ● ● ● ● ● ● ●

A potbelly would be improved by "beer and hot
dog therapy."

● ● ● ● ● ● ● ● ● ● ● ● ● ● ● ● ● ● ●

"Give-it-to-someone-who-deserves-it-more-
therapy" would cure the flu.

● ● ● ● ● ● ● ● ● ● ● ● ● ● ● ● ● ● ●

Violence would be cured by
gun control therapy.

● ● ● ● ● ● ● ● ● ● ● ● ● ● ● ● ● ●

Treatment for ugliness would be
"eat-until-you-feel-better-therapy."

● ● ● ● ● ● ● ● ● ● ● ● ● ● ● ● ● ●

If life were fair, psychosis could be cured by a
good nap, and occupational therapy would be a
30-year vacation.

● ● ● ● ● ● ● ● ● ● ● ● ● ● ● ● ● ●

Some suggested ways we can make life more fair

Require an annual lottery to pick marriage
partners, so the same people don't have the good
ones the whole time.

● ● ● ● ● ● ● ● ● ● ● ● ● ● ● ● ● ●

In alphabetical order, everyone gets to be
president for one day.

● ● ● ● ● ● ● ● ● ● ● ● ● ● ● ● ● ●

Everyone gets their turn being mugged every
couple of years.

Each team, even New Orleans, gets to win the super bowl once every 26 years.

• • • • • • • • • • • • • • • • • •

All the very attractive girls would be required to wear bad hair, strange make-up and silly clothes.

• • • • • • • • • • • • • • • • • •

We could pass a law requiring everyone to be smart.

• • • • • • • • • • • • • • • • • •

Both men and women could be required to grow facial hair.

• • • • • • • • • • • • • • • • • •

If we wanted to be fair, we would require EVERYONE to drive with a cell phone hanging from her ear.

• • • • • • • • • • • • • • • • • •

We could pass a law that nobody has to live in the Middle East...or in Oregon against his will.

• • • • • • • • • • • • • • • • • •

Rich people would have to use the same lawyers as poor people.

• • • • • • • • • • • • • • • • • •

To make life fair, we would either have to figure out a way to make math a whole lot easier, or else abolish it altogether.

●●●●●●●●●●●●●●●●●●●

All the brightest students would have their mouths wired shut and take medication to muddle their thinking in order to level the playing field.

 # Many experts believe that life is not fair

"If you want to live longer, give up all the things that make you want to live longer"

- Old Bavarian Adage

A few years ago I discovered a sad fact: I can't buy everything I want to buy. This is absolutely not fair. Why should Howard Hughes be able to buy Spruce Gooses, tropical islands, and entire governments all the time having been dead for many years, while I can barely pay attention? Why should my wife have to delay buying me the luxury condominium and Leer Jet in Tahiti so she can afford to get me a pair of socks for my birthday, at the same time Mrs. Bill Gates, is charging her purchase of the entire Turks and Caicos island chain on her American Express Card? Do you call this fair? I think not. When it comes to money, then, one must conclude that life clearly is not fair.

I have pondered this lack of financial fairness for many years, particularly those years when I have had to fight off bill collectors with a hair dryer and a weed eater, or pay one credit card bill with another credit card, and I have discovered some immutable financial truths:

Immutable Financial Truth #1

Most people who have more money than me are dirty, low down skunks.

It's true. Rich people send their kids to the finest private schools where they are coddled by the finest teachers, taught to play uppity European sports like lacrosse, horse polo, and that "how many students they can cram into a Volkswagen" game, all the while being spared the trauma of eating school lunch or having the big kid on the football team leave cleatmarks up their collective sternums.

My kids, on the other hand go to the public schools where they are taught the finer points of putting fake vomit on Mr. Snarr's chemistry table, the art of being sure to schedule Algebra from the easy teacher, and how to get the library computers to change low reading grades to an A.

People richer than me get their ill-gotten gain by cashing my utility bills and house payments, by coming up with disgusting Rapp lyrics, dodging their fair share of taxes, or by being a politician in New Jersey.

The rest of us have to try to compete by having garage sales and lobbying our kids to conserve toilet paper. This is not fair.

Immutable Financial Truth #2

The reason why I'm not rich enough to be considered a dirty, low down skunk is not because of a lack of intelligence or ambition. It is largely due to the well known international conspiracy[1] to keep me in poverty.

This first point needs emphasis. Everyone knows that evil, conniving, greedy rich people, are allowed every day to exploit the downtrodden working classes, to trash the environment, scoff at the homeless, and generally thumb their noses at society's

---

[1] I try to appeal to a broad audience. Since there are millions of you out there who pretty much explain everything by blaming it onto an "international conspiracy", it seems prudent to me to try to cash in on this trend as a way to expand my readership base. Those of you who are really sharp have already grasped my thinly veiled attempt to patronize this focus group. Way to go. Pat yourselves on the back.

laws and conventions. Lord knows I certainly would love to be able to exploit the poor working class, trash the environment, and thumb my nose at society's laws[2]. But, thanks to this conspiracy, I will probably never have the chance. And yet politicians never seem to feel my pain.

Immutable Financial Truth #3

Every time I get one puny freckle of my financial proboscis above the water line, some dirty, low down skunk will symbolically stick a dirt clod into my nostril, or else some figurative tsunami will financially pin my wallet under an old tire on the symbolic ocean floor.

A few years ago, I was working for a company which seemed as happy as a puppy on new carpet with my performance. I was going places. I was as excited as a Rolaids salesman at a chili cook-off anticipating a nice promotion and an obscene raise to go with it. Unfortunately, the week before I got this raise, the contractor finished our new house and I had no choice but to replace the construction loan with permanent financing, which financing cost us the exact amount of our raise, plus a few bucks.

Not too long after this, I was promised another promotion. We were as excited as a weasel on

---

[2]Listen, I know Steve Martin used a line pretty much like this in some movie a few years ago. I felt it was a good enough line to be used twice.

amphetamines[3] looking like we would finally have enough money to super-size our happy meals. But as luck would have it at roughly the same time as we got our raise, the first payment on our shiny, new Gremlin came due. And so it has gone pretty much throughout my life. I just hope probate on Mom and Dad's estate goes through fast enough so I can use our share of the money to cover the recreational property I just bought.

---

[3]Hey, I was excited, OK? How would you describe it?

Some observers have observed that life is rarely fair

"No matter what happens there's always someone who knew it would"

- Rusty Cannon

14-reasons why men are superior to cats (Some women prefer cats to men. We think this is unfair. Therefore, we made this list)

1. Men don't cough up fur balls on your furniture.

●●●●●●●●●●●●●●●●●●●

2. Men normally don't leave partly eaten mouse parts lying around the yard.

• • • • • • • • • • • • • • • • • •

3. Beating men at video games can be a fun challenge. I certainly wouldn't brag about beating my cat.

• • • • • • • • • • • • • • • • • •

4. When they do throw up, men sometimes make it to the toilet.

• • • • • • • • • • • • • • • • • •

5. Men make much better fishing buddies.

• • • • • • • • • • • • • • • • • •

6. If you step on a man who's lying curled up on your floor in the middle of the night, he won't scream and scratch your eyes out.

• • • • • • • • • • • • • • • • • •

7. Their scratch boxes don't make your whole house smell.

• • • • • • • • • • • • • • • • • •

8. When a guy doesn't come home at night, maybe it's because he's been working.

• • • • • • • • • • • • • • • • • •

9. Men don't shed all summer long.

• • • • • • • • • • • • • • • • • •

10. They can operate a T.V. remote.

• • • • • • • • • • • • • • • • • •

11. The parasites he brings home won't multiply all through your carpet.

• • • • • • • • • • • • • • • • • •

12. Guys sometimes call.

• • • • • • • • • • • • • • • • • •

13. Pull on a cat's finger; nothing happens.

• • • • • • • • • • • • • • • • • •

14. He has some practical uses besides mousing and target practice.

 # It very well could be that life is just unfair

"While poor personal hygiene won't help a chicken socially, it may boost her life expectancy."
                                    - Biff Disraeli

The cult of the evil parents

I don't know about the rest of you parents out there, but I love being a parent. What I love most is the feeling of absolute power and control. I know of no greater satisfaction than watching a respectful teen bow in humble reverence and jump at his parent's every command, especially in a place that has a real low ceiling. I must admit, sometimes I am tempted to abuse this enormous power by demanding my kids scurry around bumping into each other.

A few years ago, my kids and some of their friends got onto this whining kick, complaining about how they were so picked on. So a group of parenting friends and I got together and formed a lobbying group to counter their whining and to pool our resources so we could hire a lawyer in case they sued. We also wanted to bond with other parents who haven't had a good nights sleep since their kid was in fifth-grade. We called our group "The Cult of the Evil Parents." This group's main function, as the name implies, is to give mean, rotten parents an excuse to get together a couple of times a month, dance naked around a bon fire, stick pins into dolls of their children, and think up ways to ruin all their kids' fun.

OK, maybe that's not exactly what we do, but that's what my kids think. I admit that my wife and I do make our kids sometimes clean their rooms and wash the dishes, and I do have a dump-truck-load of contempt for wimpy, wishy-washy, or lazy parents who lack the gumption to stand up to their kids, because they make my job so much harder. This is not fair.

Therefore, for those parents whose kids are the "everybody else's" that my kids are always talking about, I offer:

How to be a mean Mom or Dad

Rules of the cult

Rule#1. OK. I admit it. We have no rules.

Rule #2. We have no idea what we're doing.

Rule #3. In fact, technically, the cult does not even exist yet; however, I don't think that should stop us from making a little bit of money off the idea.

Therefore, for parents who have learned everything they know about parenting by watching Ozzie Ozbourne, yet, surprisingly, still have spoiled, rebellious, disobedient children, we have put together a series of parenting tool packages to help rehabilitate you.

You may notice how expensive these packages are. That's because they are "brand name" packages and we figure anyone dumb enough to buy one of them is certainly stupid enough to pay a comically high price for them too. Accept no substitutes.

Tools for spineless parents

Package #1 sells for only $1,999.00. It was designed for parents who can't say No!" It includes a recording of your child emphatically repeating "No! No! No!" over and over again when he was a toddler and you were trying to get him to eat squash, and it has a pause in between each one. Just listen carefully, and during the pause between No's, repeat the word "No" until you have the confidence to use it in your every day vocabulary. Don't be discouraged. You'll get the hang of it eventually.

As a bonus, we will include some recordings of assorted college admittance committees, bank loan officers, potential employers, and parole officers repeating the word, "no, no, no, no, no," over and over again. While the significance of this will be lost on your child, if YOU listen to the tapes, implement a well-planned exercise program, and take calcium supplements, in the long run it could actually strengthen your spine.

Package #2 sells for $2,999.00. It is designed for parents who are too busy, who feel they have more important things to do than raise their child, or who are just plain not interested. It consists of a pregnancy termination kit that should work even on pregnancies as late as the 39th trimester. Many of these embryos will now be in junior high. It is a simple machine made up of a skateboard and a homing device, which locks onto the nearest semi truck or cliff.

Package #3 is only $3,999.00. Let's say you feel that being a friend to your child is more important than being a parent. Maybe you feel he or she is getting more than enough guidance and limits in the public schools and by watching the Simpsons. This package starts with a pair of loner parents for you AND for your kids. You will also receive a matching set of stuffed Care Bears, and a 900 hot line to call anytime day or night whenever you or your child needs a friend. (I should point out that the phone service costs an extra $50.00 a minute.)

Package #4 The deluxe package is only $4,999.00. This is for parents who fear they are on shaky moral ground to place limitations on their kids because of mistakes they made when they were younger. The package contains a canteen full of water, a bag of trail mix, a change of underwear, a one-way ticket to Saudi Arabia, and a 25-year supply of birth control pills.

It may occur to you that by buying any of these packages you have bought the equivalent of a luxury cruise to North Dakota, or that you now own beach front property in Wyoming. This is true. Many of these packages cost ten-times more money than they are actually worth. Don't get all worked up; it is supposed to be like that. This gross overpricing is an essential part of your therapy. Being hammered like this will prepare you for the neglect and abandonment you will experience in a few years when your kids stick you in a nursing home so they can party with your money.

So, there you have it. As I see it, if you are a parent, you have only two choices: #1, get out your credit card, look over this product list, find the package that is just right for you…or, #2, get mean and grab a loincloth. The meetings are on Tuesday nights.

Scientific evidence is beginning to suggest that life is not fair

"Stupidity is like earwax: you don't mind having it as long as people can't see it."

- Brodie Satva

Health is not fair

According to millions of TV and radio ads, the greatest blessing one can have, the most precious treasure in a guy's life should be his hair. If you don't have enough, you are now required by law to have low self-esteem, women are not allowed to think you're sexy, people shouldn't hire you, and you're a higher risk for an early death due to being mistaken for a wrecking ball, or getting a loser part in a sit com, or because of suicide.

37

As attractive and sexy as a luxurious head of hair is, I would like to point out that it's hard to strut around gloating and acting condescending to bald guys if you're hovering near death from leprosy, your family has left you because they're tired of hiding out from the Marines who are closing in on your bunker, your brain is about to fall out because of advanced gingivitis, or you're spending the winter on the streets of Chicago because you're a heroin addict...or you're dead. Therefore, although I would concur that a guy's hair should be the most important thing in his life, I would have to consider health a close second. Thus, I feel it my journalistic duty to instruct my readers in some of the secrets of good health.

The secret of good health

A big (no pun intended) problem with health is obesity, or as most health professionals affectionately call it, "fluffiness." Experts tell us that chronic chubbiness is the cause of many other health problems such as losing one's balance and falling backward off a cliff, having to buy extra-large bikinis, being eaten by Eskimos who think you're a walrus, and catching your sagging arm skin on the car mirror.

I admit I have a problem with my weight as a result of an eating disorder I had as a youth. As a teenager, from April, 1964, through September, 1972, never once was I full. Don't blame my mom either; she tried. Mom processed meals like a third-world hospital septic system in the middle of a dysentery epidemic[1]. And the stuff would pour into me like water up the nose of a fallen water skier with the rope wrapped around his ankle[2].

And I was skinny too. No doubt my metabolism could have kept pace at the time with an auctioneer on amphetamines[3].

This eating habit established as a young man has caused severe psychological problems. Whenever I go in for my humiliating annual physical where jolly doctors probe around my body orifices, I see the chart of normal height and weight, which causes me to become depressed. As many of you know, depression in most people causes them to try to eat their way out of the condition craving ice cream, chocolate, and cheese sticks. So I'm stuck on this vicious treadmill, which unfortunately is only a symbolic treadmill, which, if it was an actual treadmill, I could get jogging and maybe lose some weight.

---

[1] Although what I am using here is a common writers' technique known as hyperbole, it's probably best to point out that this simile, while certainly a clever literary device, is purely figurative and should not be taken literally, especially as it relates to my Mom's cooking. Hi Mom!

[2] I should know. This happened to me once.

[3] Since I seem to be having a bad analogy day, I guess I better apologize to all my readers who are auctioneers or who are on amphetamines, or who are in some other way connected with auctions or amphetamines, as well as to anyone else who plans to become an auctioneer or to be on amphetamines.

39

More about breakfast

Life is not fair. I love breakfast. It's my favorite meal. And the great thing is the experts tell us it's the most important meal of the day. The problem, as I'm sure you're aware, is that everything good for breakfast will kill you. Even though I understand this perfectly, I should admit that if the time ever comes that I have to eat a healthy breakfast, I will begin to hate breakfast. This could cause me to miss the most important meal of the day.

Many people delude themselves into believing they really like kelp and garlic bagels, egg substitutes, and water. Any dead Greek philosopher would tell you (if he could talk) that the ultimate lie is a lie to oneself. Therefore, in order to hang on to what little mental health I have, I must avoid guilt from eating unhealthy breakfasts, and yet, at the same time, have a rational philosophy. I have a simple but effective way of doing this. I blame someone else.

In the case of my unhealthy chubbiness, logically I choose to blame the tobacco industry. They are world-class villains. When people quit smoking, since food tastes better and they have various nervous twitches, they nearly always gain weight. Since I have never smoked, my appetite has been outstanding for my whole life. Since I know that taking up smoking, especially being overweight already, would most likely kill me, I have no choice but to stay with my program of not smoking which, as outlined above, is the cause of my gaining weight.

This is probably a good time for another food-related observation. It's clearly not fair that kids, at least the ones I know, generally don't even care about any of this. Breakfast to them is not a big deal. They don't worry about cholesterol. They don't think about their metabolisms. They don't even like the good stuff they're not supposed to eat. Ironically, a Denver omelet with Tabasco sauce, sausage, eggs fried in sausage grease, or biscuits and sausage gravy are all legal for them. With their squirrel metabolisms, fat and cholesterol have no chance. This is clearly not fair.

Life isn't fair, yet nobody cares

"The red fern didn't grow over petroleum-based nitrogen granules."

- Mildred Flummox

One of life's great contradictions is that everyone has problems, yet no one cares...about others' problems, that is. If you doubt this, or think you're different, do some research: take a poll. Ask people, "I have some problems. Do you care? Would you like to hear about my problems?"

Since now you're all suicidal because of this revelation, I'm sure you are now asking yourself, "Is there anything I can do to make myself feel better?" To which I would answer, "Do chickens have lips? Is the Pope Catholic?" Do snakes have armpits?

Regardless of how you answered these questions, I must say that you CAN feel better. You can get a pet. Never mind that your pet cares even less than the humans around you, because fortunately for your emotional well being, your pet has had 10,000 years of careful breeding which have engineered the puppy or kitty so she instinctively SEEMS to be hanging onto your every word and ACTS as though she cares, even though your words make about as much sense to her as the sound of the rocks rattling around in your hubcaps. For your pet, acting like he is enraptured by your voice has kept him from being eaten through all these generations of evolution. And it gets him food.

I know that some of you who are too smart to waste your energy talking to your pet, or who have made a decision to go through life without having fur balls in the cracks of your furniture and bacteria-encrusted liter boxes at the foot of your bed, need to feel like SOMEBODY out there cares about you. You would like an alternative to pet ownership. If you would like an alternative to talking to animals, the good news is that you can always put your lively imagination to work. The act of visualizing someone goofier than a doorstop made of linguini can sometimes make an emotionally unstable person feel a little better.

44

For example, let's say the judge just demanded that you give up your drivers' license and that the bailiff, whispering to you in his announcer's voice, just notified the entire courtroom that you have head lice. While you are being humiliated and demeaned by the court and while you are giving your drivers license back to the judge, if you want to feel better, you can check out of reality. You can maintain your good feelings and even get a good chuckle by visualizing this mean judge failing to check the depth of the water beneath the rock he's jumping off from while wearing a speed-o, or you can imagine that HIS head lice are having a race to see who can be the fastest to burrow to the center of his head. The judge will have no idea you're doing this. He will be busy patting himself on the back for getting another loony person off the street. And you will be having a great time and improving your outlook on life.

Bragging

This chapter about caring people would not be complete if we didn't also mention the fact that even when you manage to accomplish something good, even amazing, nobody cares. And, unfortunately, if you want to make people recognize your accomplishments by bragging about yourself, people will consider you a boorish, disgusting barbarian with sub human interpersonal skills. Still, by the time someone else gets around to saying something about your wonderfulness, you will be on the old mausoleum-smelling funeral pyre floating to Valhalla.

So, some useful ideas about bragging are probably in order here. It's not fair that whenever you do something you consider outstanding, you can't brag about it, especially since no one else will brag for you because they don't care. And you have to be pretty careful here, because if you brag about yourself, people might mistake you for a pro athlete or something. That can be bad, since as everyone knows, being mistaken for a pro athlete is like advertising to the world that you're a self-centered, greedy, immature, spoiled, world-class boorish, dope-smoking backside of a horse. So, like most people, when you do something good, you can sit around with a smug, odd smile on your face hoping that someone will notice and actually care, you can brag about it yourself (also not a good idea as explained above), or you can read on and discover a pretty good third option, which you probably had never considered.

A pretty good third option

If you happen to find yourself in a position where you need to brag about something you did, and you can't play a pro sport where it's understood that you're self indulgent, immature, braggart, because so few pro sports want 50-year old paunchy slugs who frequently throw their backs out while shaving, and who would likely struggle through a 160 game season, and who don't want to take steroids or smoke dope, or who are self-conscious about adjusting their crotches in front of 8 million fans. So, many of us are left with only one responsible alternative: VENTRILOQUISM. Yes, imagine how cool it would be to make up your own compliments and have them seem as though they were coming from someone of significance. Hey, even if you throw your voice, catching an important person completely off guard and they get mad because they know they didn't say what they said, what's an important person going to do after some smarmy compliment comes out of his mouth, deny he said it? I don't think so.

If you're rotten at throwing your voice, you can sometimes get an even better effect by hiding speakers and playing pre-recorded celebrity messages about your wonderfulness by remote control. This has the advantage that people will believe they are actually hearing celebrities praise you. Imagine the thrill of receiving regular sincere compliments from Dan Rather, Colin Powell or Woody Allen!

 Many people have noticed that life is sometimes not fair

"If you did it, try really hard not to draw attention to yourself, and try not to look guilty while leaving quickly"

- Old Trial Lawyers' Saying

Times have changed. I remember when home security consisted of a dog and a shotgun. And they worked fine. My uncle Jack has the hides of a few dozen former burglars tacked on his shed to prove it. Many of you older readers have memories of the times when a standard, garden-variety stupid burglar would be breaking into your house, going through your kitchen window, and Sparky would take a big bite out of his backside just before you shot him. (Some of you may even have pictures.)

Unfortunately, today Fifi can't and won't do the kind of blue-collar home security and defense that Sparky did in times past. Besides that, now-days, a homeowner also has to worry about being sued by the heirs of the dead burglar if he bleeds to death on someone else's property. And then if you add to this the problems of bewildering technology, more sophisticated criminals, and psychotic judges from distant planets, the times require extraordinary measures undreamed of just a few short years ago. For some of you, it's not even safe to keep guns around any more because you have to worry that people might think you were planning to go hunt animals with the intent of eating them or something. No, it's safer today to just eat chicken nuggets. So, just what do you do?

For your family's safety, I recommend one of the following three options

Option #1

First, you can hire a security company. If you're like me, from time to time you have probably received advertisements in the mail informing you that you're house is 10 times more likely than your neighbors to be robbed because you are the only family within a 7-light year radius who hasn't installed this company's alarm system, and further warning you that if you don't buy their system, they're going to stick a little sign in all of their customers' lawns announcing to all would-be burglars that your home is open and unprotected if they want to give it a try. So, you can call them and for just a little more than the price of a used Space Shuttle they will come by and install a sophisticated alarm system, which will sense any motion within your house and summon them to rush to arrest you as you break into your own fridge. They will also install heavy-duty dead bolt locks to keep your kids from getting into the house after school, and, of course, they will stick a little sign in your lawn referring all the thieves to any home in your neighborhood who doesn't pay for their security system.

Option #2

Another alternative is to move to a gated community. I have a sister who lives in a gated community, and so I can speak with some authority when I say that moving into a house in a gated community will make you and your male relatives very tired, especially the piano. I can also state with some authority that gated communities possess some other advantages. For example, everyone will think you are rich, especially if you tell them that rickety '88 Chrysler parked on top of the oil slick in your driveway is a classic 007 movie car that you're going to be restoring soon. Another advantage is having a frail 92-year-old blind, deaf guy guarding the gate, only letting the thieves, terrorists, and pests inside who are able to drop an important sounding name or sneak in while he is having his nap.

Option #3

Finally, if all these options are too pricey, you can use the poor mans' approach: Booby traps. I can best illustrate the advantages of this option by using a personal experience.

Unfortunately, I don't have any personal experience. That shouldn't, however, stop you from considering the use of booby traps to protect your property and loved ones. Visualize, if you will, a doped up potential killer strung out on cocaine, cough syrup, glue, and Pepto Bismol sneaking past your '88 Chrysler and tripping a wire which throws a switch that turns on a car stereo system with super bass speakers. This will wake up the entire neighborhood. Some of your neighbors will be so cranky they will kill him for you.

More evidence that life is not fair

If life were fair, we would all be equally good looking.

....

If life were fair, fish could leave the water whenever their fingers got wrinkly.

....

If life were fair, chickens, pigs, and cows would get to eat people some of the time.

....

If life were fair, the best player would get to bat for both teams.

....

If life were fair, chocolate wouldn't make your face break out.

....

If life were fair, it wouldn't always rain for a few days after you wash your car.

....

If life were fair, you would get better looking and healthier as you get older.

There are times when life clearly seems unfair

"If you don't want to lose, don't pick on someone your own size"

- Napoleon or somebody

Automated answering machines are from the devil

It isn't fair that a person can never speak to another live person any more. Let's say you own a terrific business. It's thriving; it's growing; you are getting rich providing a product or service that the public needs and wants. Then one day, maybe your medication gets all messed up, or maybe you are inexplicably overwhelmed with a desire to feel pain.

55

Maybe, you want to be poor for a while because you can't remember what it was like. Whatever your hypothetical reasons, one day you decide to see how angry you can make all your customers; you want to see if, in just a few days, you can kill something that took you years of hard work and sacrifice to build.

Thanks to experiences you've had in the past, many of you are already ahead of me here. Without even thinking, you intuitively know a simple way to do this: You can install an automated answering service!

It is entirely possible that YOU, my deranged reader, are planning to set up an automated answering system at YOUR business tomorrow. Before you pass the point of no return, take a deep breath. Consider: maybe your customers aren't such awful people after all; maybe YOU'RE just having a bad day or suffering from some fundamental mechanical flaw in your judgment, from menopausal hot flashes, from post-traumatic stress syndrome, or from benign brain flatulence. Take a deep breath. Don't do anything rash. These feelings may pass. Maybe you'll feel differently tomorrow.

In order to keep you, our judgmentally challenged reader from making a rotten, life-altering mistake, we here at Apricot Press want to get you thinking by offering some alternatives. Instead of installing automated telephone answering systems, if you really want to see how angry and frustrated you can make all of your customers, consider one of these strategies instead. Some of them will work almost as well:

You could save a lot of hassle by simply hiring
an arsonist to burn your
business down.

● ● ● ● ● ● ● ● ● ● ● ● ● ● ● ● ●

Instead, why not announce a policy that
your company hires only ex-cons,
child molesters, and convicted gangsters
to deal with the public.

● ● ● ● ● ● ● ● ● ● ● ● ● ● ● ● ●

You could commit corporate suicide when
you stop making large contributions
to key politicians'
campaign war chests.

● ● ● ● ● ● ● ● ● ● ● ● ● ● ● ● ●

I know; call a news conference to announce that
for the past few years your business has been
nothing but a sophisticated front for terrorism.
Announce further that you are planning to get
together with all the anti American defense
lawyers, college professors, and Ted Turner to
make a strategy to bring down the entire
corporate infrastructure so that we can all live in
peace and harmony under a tyrannical central
government modeled after Pakistan, who will
cane or shoot us whenever we are suspected of
thinking something harmful to the ruling junta.

Re-name your company some vicious, insulting Native American name such as the "Indians" or "Braves."

●●●●●●●●●●●●●●●●●●

Advertise that all your products now include the following ingredients: Anthrax, E-Bola spores, tobacco and Big Macs.

●●●●●●●●●●●●●●●●●●

Publicize your new corporate policy of providing substandard service for all minorities and women, and in all advertising, whenever the company refers to one of these groups, make it a point to use a demeaning slur.

●●●●●●●●●●●●●●●●●●

Go ahead. If you are determined to trash your business, instead of running with the herd and using automated answering machinery like everyone else, be original; try one of these techniques. They should be nearly as effective and you'll save the investment in expensive equipment.

More evidence that life is not fair

If life were fair, there would be no short
people...or all short people.

• • • • • • • • • • • • • • • • • •

If life were fair, cows would also get
to milk people.

• • • • • • • • • • • • • • • • • •

If life were fair, onions wouldn't give you
heartburn or bad breath.

• • • • • • • • • • • • • • • • • •

If life were fair, rabbits would get to eat
coyotes their share of the time.

• • • • • • • • • • • • • • • • • •

If life were fair, the weeds would also get to
poison the people some of the time.

• • • • • • • • • • • • • • • • • •

If life were fair, everyone would have his own
Nintendo 64.

Life often seems to be unfair

"Whenever you are in deep caca, it's best to keep
your mouth shut."
- Felix Del Gato

On Cussing

When it comes to cussing, life is not fair. Recently,
while in a neighboring state on business, I was
overpowered by an urge to eat a dead chicken.
Naturally, I went to a nearby K.F.C. to get some.
While waiting in line, I was shocked to hear the
language coming from a clot of adolescents. Among
other things, they were loudly describing immoral
acts using words I hadn't heard since I played college
football. In this group, besides obnoxious guys, were
a bunch of tender, young women. And even though

these young women were dressed like they were getting ready to storm Dracula's castle, and looked as though they could whup the boys, they were still young women...I think.

I was shocked, nay, chagrined, that they seemed to understand many of the words the guys were using; I know I did. And if not the words, they couldn't help but understand the tone and attitude, which from what I was hearing would have caused docile, arthritic, old dogs to launch into berserk attack mode. In fact, standing there listening to them began to make ME want to cuss, but I knew if I did cuss in front of the ladies, my dad would somehow find out, appear out of nowhere, and kick my butt. (Can we say "butt" in this book?)

I'll bet I'm not the only old person who's had an experience like this with cussing. I'll bet that many of my readers are often confused about the new rules that apply to cussing, which seem to have been imposed without getting older peoples' permission. Many of my readers may also be confused about the substantial legal risks and penalties for cussing at incorrect times. So, since the rules have changed so much in the past few years, and since messing this one up can land you in jail or cause special interest groups to chain themselves and their lawyers to your house or business, I provide you the following information. If you ever plan to cuss, we suggest you memorize this.

Cussing is now legal when:

*Provided no children are present.

Whenever you're acting in a movie or on TV.

● ● ● ● ● ● ● ● ● ● ● ● ● ● ● ● ● ●

If you're a lead singer in a rock
or rapp group.

● ● ● ● ● ● ● ● ● ● ● ● ● ● ● ● ● ●

When you're a drill sergeant.

● ● ● ● ● ● ● ● ● ● ● ● ● ● ● ● ● ●

Whenever you're changing your oil and you
accidentally screw the tip of your thumb into
the oil filter hole.

● ● ● ● ● ● ● ● ● ● ● ● ● ● ● ● ● ●

When a referee makes a bad call against
your team.

● ● ● ● ● ● ● ● ● ● ● ● ● ● ● ● ● ●

When you are the President of the United States
and all of your conversations about bugging the
opposing political party's offices are being
recorded.

● ● ● ● ● ● ● ● ● ● ● ● ● ● ● ● ● ●

You are a low-life, reprobate,
scummy dirt bag.

You are a professional athlete or coach
and the TV camera is focused on a
tight shot of your face.

••••••••••••••••••

When addressing a stubborn, block-headed,
brain-dead animal such as a cow, mule, or
telemarketer.

Cussing can be bad when:

On family home videos or movies.

••••••••••••••••••

In front of your grandma.

••••••••••••••••••

While speaking to a Sunday school class.

••••••••••••••••••

During the sentencing phase of your trial.

Modern cussing paradoxes:

Boy cusses in front of Mom. Mom washes boy's
mouth out with soap.

Boy cusses at girl. Boy gets date.

• • • • • • • • • • • • • • • • • •

Girl cusses in front of Mom. Girl gets grounded and has to ride bus to school.

• • • • • • • • • • • • • • • • • •

Girl cusses at boy. Girl becomes popular.

• • • • • • • • • • • • • • • • • •

Actor cusses on TV. Ratings improve; kids impatiently await the next episode.

• • • • • • • • • • • • • • • • • •

Boy cusses at boy. Bonding occurs.

• • • • • • • • • • • • • • • • • •

Girl cusses at girl. Cat-fight ensues.

• • • • • • • • • • • • • • • • • •

Middle-aged white male cusses in presence of women. Middle-aged white male receives 30-year prison term for sexual harassment.

• • • • • • • • • • • • • • • • • •

Ethnic minority cusses in presence of white females and males. Ethnic minority gets paid millions as stand up comedian.

Middle aged white male cusses in front of minorities. Middle-aged white male gets sued for discrimination.

• • • • • • • • • • • • • • • • • •

Middle-aged white male cusses at cows. Cows ignore middle-aged white male and continue being stupid

• • • • • • • • • • • • • • • • • •

New words, which have recently become swear words, which didn't used to be:

Category 1 forbidden words: Gender-based personal pronouns. You are absolutely forbidden from ever using derogative, stereotyping words like, "he", and "she' in public.

Example #1: Wrong: "How did you ever fool her, that hot, sexy girl, into marrying you?"

Right: "How did you convince that beautiful and intelligent person to marry you?"

Example #2: Wrong: "If you don't bend your knees and guard your man, an impression of the wood pattern from the end of the bench will become a permanent tattoo on your back side."

Right: "Would you please guard your <u>person</u>!?"

Example #3: Wrong: "If men's brains were nuclear fuel and you were to gather them all together there wouldn't be enough energy to cook a wiener."

Right: "There are many intellectually disadvantaged <u>persons</u> out there."

Another formerly common word, which is now illegal is the word, "Retard." I don't know about you, but my friends and I used to call everyone a "retard." Holy cow! Don't try this today!

* There are many new words added each day to the forbidden list. Watch it.

Maybe it has occurred to you that life is not fair

"Sometimes life can be as simple
as catching a nap while riding on
a motorcycle."

- Eric Nid

Fatness and Fairness

If you're fat, life is not fair. Through no fault of their
own, plump people take an enormous amount of
abuse, maybe even more than Corporate C.E.Os,
cigarette smokers, or possibly even carnivores. This
is clearly not fair.

There are perfectly good people out there who, for some odd reason, fat wants no part of. They eat a breakfast of two donuts, hot chocolate, éclairs, and cinnamon rolls. They do no exercise, unless you consider fidgeting. They have a mid day snack of pastries and gummy bears and a hamburger lunch, and yet are still so skinny they can get through a screen door without opening it, so skinny seagulls don't waste their time. Their household appliances look like they have an eating disorder out of sympathy. You get the picture. I, on the other hand, get fat just thinking of cheese sticks. I gain weight on distilled water, oxygen, and Styrofoam peanuts. This is clearly not fair.

From the looks of your thighs, I can see that you are just like me, or worse. This is not fair. So, fortunately, I have thought of some good solutions. For example, in order to even the playing field for corpulent people versus the flat bellies, figuratively, we could start by getting some good legal representation for the plump and rotund. One good way to start would be to create a non-profit organization of nasty, evil lawyers, who would fight in behalf of all the "chubby" people in the world. We should model this group after the tobacco lobby. The nice thing about having our own chunkiness lobby is we wouldn't have to lie or exaggerate about how tough things are because the lawyers would do it all for us. They love that stuff. They can lurk around, and every time they hear a disparaging comment about someone's weight or girth, voila!

They're zeroed in on millions of dollars in punitive damages.

And we could have some business watchdogs, too. Any time a fluffy person doesn't get a promotion, is fired, or isn't hired, we can blame it on chubbiness discrimination.

Getting the message out

Somehow we've got to get the message out that it's expensive for those of us who are fluffy. Our clothes require more material. Our refrigerators need more capacity. We must have larger mirrors, and our cheeks demand more cellulite. We have to pay people to do things like tie our shoes, find our belts and ride our horses.

To better educate the public, I say we need a windfall profit tax on anyone with less than 12% body fat so we could use the money to create TV and billboard ads illustrating Rush Limbaugh trying to bend over and pick up a quarter, or Oprah or Rosie O'Donnell collapsing at the top of the stairs. The theme of the campaign could be, "There aren't enough moo moos for them all."

Some fields are terrible. Take gymnastics for instance; when was the last time you saw a gymnast who couldn't fit into an airline seat? And look at magazine covers. What percentage of people who grace the cover of Cosmopolitan weigh over 300 pounds? There's no way that the percentage of scale-smashers on magazine covers even approaches the percentage of the population at large. This can't possibly be right! I demand legislation forcing skinny basketball players to stuff some rocks into their saggy pants to put them on equal footing with their high-flying competitors. If life is ever to be fair, we must demand proportionate representation with the population of chubby people.

Unlike other special interest groups, and in spite of the way it may seem, we people with low metabolisms don't seek superiority over flat bellies; we just want equality, just to be accepted. For this to happen, there needs to be some all rotund TV shows and movies. We can create an oversight-watchdog group to monitor TV shows to guarantee compliance.

If enough money could be applied to medical research, it might allow doctors to finally dissect a few skinny people so they could begin to understand why they are like that. With enough money, I bet doctors could even transplant skinny peoples' metabolisms into the thighs of chubby people so they would look more like super models. To fund this, let's hire a celebrity to host a telethon. I recommend Roseanne Barr; her career has been in the tank for a while.

Of course, all these are just small steps. Our ultimate goal is to solve the problem once and for all. Hopefully, our efforts will end in legislation that would force fat to treat everyone with dignity and equality. As far as I'm concerned, this would help to make life fair.

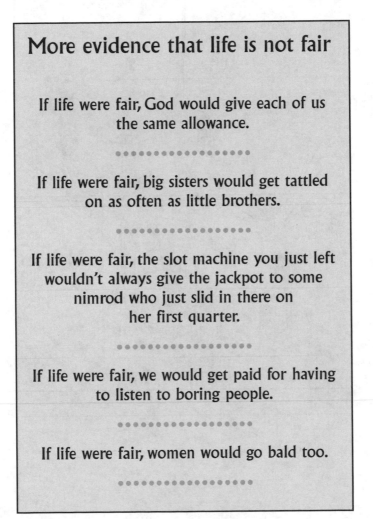

More evidence that life is not fair

If life were fair, God would give each of us the same allowance.

●●●●●●●●●●●●●●●●●●

If life were fair, big sisters would get tattled on as often as little brothers.

●●●●●●●●●●●●●●●●●●

If life were fair, the slot machine you just left wouldn't always give the jackpot to some nimrod who just slid in there on her first quarter.

●●●●●●●●●●●●●●●●●●

If life were fair, we would get paid for having to listen to boring people.

●●●●●●●●●●●●●●●●●●

If life were fair, women would go bald too.

●●●●●●●●●●●●●●●●●●

Often it
seems that
life is not fair

'If you ask enough people, you can usually find someone who will advise you what you were going to do anyway"

- Cal A. Bunga

When compared with the rich and decadent, some of us have a generously disproportionate lack of talent. But, in this unfair world, rewards, for some reason, are not distributed strictly based on talent. Take rock bands for example.

As a young whippersnapper, inspired by the Beatles, Elvis, The Rollin' Stones, Ray Stevens, and Tiny Tim, my buddies and I decided we could make it big as a rock band. While it was hard to put our finger exactly onto the ruptured artery of success, by a thorough study of the scantily clad, bizarre alien humanoids gracing our album covers and of the music and lyrics on them, we slowly began to suspect that the only talent possessed by many of the bands was a bad attitude.

We struggled to comprehend how it was that their parents let them say those words and act like loons. We guessed that it must be the money. Their moms and dads must be getting a kick-back or something.

History will back me up when I state that the reason for our failure wasn't because of a lack of talent. Our band, Maggot Casserole, failed because our parents didn't have liberal enough attitudes. They wouldn't let us cuss and play in bars. Bummer to have parents who were not motivated by greed.

Our band wasn't the only high-potential band that never made it. Unfortunately, history has shown that sometimes fate smiles lovingly on some low life scum and at the same time symbolically flushes out its septic holding tank on the heads of some other grasping, self-centered human refuse with similar or even superior skills. For some reason, at the same moment fate is pouring a steady fountain of illegal drug-induced bliss into the lives of one blob of decadent, self-indulgent, smelly, despicable band members, it is symbolically barfing and sneezing mutant bacteria on another one. I realize I'm being redundant here, but I really, really, really, really, really want to make the point that this topic of fairness lends itself perfectly to this type of metaphorical illustration and that life is absolutely not fair.

Maybe some of you out there in reader land have a burning desire to be rich and decadent and confrontational toward everything virtuous, along with an abundant lack of talent. Maybe some of you are thinking you might want to go into rock banding as a career so you can have a splendid time being exploited by drug dealers, environmental groups, conniving groupies, and magnates in the music industry. Before you take the leap of faith, let's seek to learn something from some successful rock bands...and some that didn't make it. (OK, I admit I don't know any successful rock bands. Hopefully there's a plethora of things we can learn from this bunch of losers.)

In order to understand the true facts surrounding the success or failure of one rock band vis-à-vis another, we decided to enjoy a nostalgic reminiscence of some old bands we knew who flopped like rancid, unsold mackerel falling off the back of a pickup truck on the way to the land fill.

Case Study #1

Post Nasal Drip was a band out of Peoria who believed with all their adolescent hearts they had a shot to make the big time and even received encouragement from their old high school band teacher, Mr. Snell. They were pioneering a new sound featuring songs that were real easy to play on the guitar. Their style was described as old time acid rock combined with overtones of new-age funk and a background of younger brothers and sisters banging pans and making annoying noises in the background. Their unique sound was also liberally sprinkled with dissonance, tone deafness, and faulty equipment.

They were making great progress toward developing seriously reprobate behavior patterns too. (They snuck some beer from the drummer's Uncle Fred.) But before the public was able to catch up with their avant-guarde lyrics, their lead singer, Alvin, got grounded for putting hydrogen peroxide combined with Nair on the family dog, Sparky. And his Dad, who viewed this as an act of ingratitude after he bought all their equipment and let them practice out behind his mink pens, pulled the plug on the band, symbolically.

Case Study #2
Weed Wacker was a country band which tried to create a truly unique sound by mimicking Eddie Rabbit. They further pursued this one-of-a-kind identity by taking a break in the middle of their show to allow Jake, their drummer, to play a few songs on his ukulele because they thought it was cool.

They insist the biggest reason for their demise was a failure to be adequately promoted. Their manager, who doubled singing back-up vocals, was angry and frustrated that "Achy Breaky Heart" was a good enough song to make a star out of one person and yet it left another perfectly good band playing anonymously in Burt's Dad's barn.

Case Study #3
The group known as Bladder Infection was enjoying a dizzying vault to the top of the charts...(of basic elements behind the stage in the Chemistry Lab), when their dreams came to an end about as abruptly as a showering guy's morning song when a prankster turns off the hot water. The reasons weren't all clear, but contributing factors were: The mean old orchestra teacher, Mr. Strange, needed his amplifier for a pep assembly, they had to take their stuff home because of the start of practice for the school play, and Herb got himself grounded for a year after turning a bunch of skunks loose at their rival school's prom.

Here are some other bands who didn't make it either, but certainly not because of a lack of attitude-or an unprofessional sounding name (We put these out there in case one of you can use them. We hate to waste perfectly good names): Macular Degeneration, Puberty Unchained, Rancid Grey Matter, Grunt, Septic Pulse, Aneurysm, Bottom of the Food Chain, Hemorrhoidal Hamburger, Sludge, Adolescent Psychosis, Swine Feed, Mega Belch and The Flatulations, Peptic Ulcer, Ragweed, Bilge Water and the Barbarians.

V.P. of Maintenance

It seems that life sometimes is really unfair

"In order for us to eat bacon, somebody has to inconvenience the pig."

- Will Knapp

Old people can remember when job titles gave the public some idea of what a person actually did. For example, it's hard to mistake what a mechanic, mailman, ditch-digger, butcher, baker, or candlestick-maker would do for you. Unfortunately, these demeaning titles were given to workers during a time when the king or queen pretty much owned everyone, and no one dared demand a more prestigious job because the king might chop off his head.

A few years ago, this all began to change. As we got farther into our sophisticated modern age the pool of prospective workers became more savvy. Now that workers could choose their own line of rotten work, most chose to wait until a job opened up in the field of presidenting, celebritying, or being heir to a large fortune. This in turn made it hard for business owners to get people to apply to do demeaning jobs that paid slave wages.

At about this time, it was most likely in some best selling positive thinking book, that a motivational speaker came up with the idea of giving cool sounding job titles to company grunts as one way to avoid having to pay them a decent wage. Before you could say, "indentured servant," every janitor in America became a "Maintenance Vice President", every construction worker became an "Excavation Engineer", every baby sitter became a "Diaper Recycler", and every javalin-catcher in America became "Vice President of Organ Perforation".

And it worked, too, for a few years. All these poorly paid workers who had to do all the rotten jobs did them with smiles on their faces while whistling happy tunes all the while thinking they were awfully darned important. Then one day, somebody let the old lint ball out of the belly button, the wolverine out of the janitor closet, the cat out of the old microwave, so to speak. Maybe it was a union boss negotiating for a higher wage; maybe it was some guy who complained that this new job kept him from ever being home to help his wife do the dishes; maybe it was a bacterial infection planted in our water by evil enemies of our way of life. Whatever the reason, low-life scum working stiffs got wise. They systematically began to rise up in rebellion. They discovered en masse that even though they had a cool job title that gave them considerable prestige with themselves, their paycheck still sucked. And once they started looking around, it wasn't long until they noticed that despite their important-sounding titles, the public and those writing their paychecks still treated them like antebellum, Southern, agricultural workers.

Upon further examination, some of the more perceptive workers noticed they were still doing pretty much the same work as they had been doing before, only, now they were on salary, which meant they worked twice as many hours and got paid in Pez. Rumor has it this discovery was made when the chairman of the snow removal board for Shedding Moose Oil Inc. of Alaska had his foot run over by a snow blower on the job and went to file his workers comp claim, which was denied because, according to OSHA, with this job title, he should have been at least two office technicians and a V.P. of refuse engineering away from any actual machinery.

The problem is now we're all confused. We're stuck with a whole slew of new funky job titles, which the public often find hard to figure out. Fortunately, we are here to disconfuse you. To help you, our confused readers, get along better in life, we have provided this translation of job titles for your use. These titles are subject to change without notice, which means that before this information gets to you, it will undoubtedly be obsolete. Void where prohibited by law.

A Translation of Trendy Job Titles

Official Title: Customer Services Representative
Translation: Sales Clerk
Actual Job: Put you on hold

Official Title: Service Technician:
Translation: Handyman
Actual Job: Explain why your warranty doesn't cover this particular defect

Official Title: Account Executive
Translation: Salesman
Actual Job: Call you at inconvenient times and persistently counter your reasons for not wanting to buy the company's product or services

Official Title: V.P. Maintenance
Translation: Janitor
Actual Job: Leans on broom exchanging anecdotes

Official Title: Landscape Engineer
Translation: Weed whacker
Actual Job: Whacks weeds.

Official Title: Corporate Law Partner
Translation: Defense Lawyer
Actual Job: Lies to get money

Official Title: Senator Sludge
Translation: Defense Lawyer
Actual Job: Lies to get money

Official Title: Governor Mundane
Translation: Defense Lawyer
Actual Job: Lies to get money

Official Title: Juvenile Activities Director
Translation: Baby sitter
Actual Job: Tends other peoples' kids

Official Title: Education Facilitator
Translation: School Teacher
Actual Job: Tends peoples' kids while ducking spit wads

Official Title: Corporate C.E.O.
Translation: The Boss
Actual Job: Figures out creative methods of increasing his own compensation package without necessarily producing any more income for his shareholders

Official Title: News Anchor
Translation: Talking Head
Actual Job: Carefully gives all the news with proper liberal slant while articulately denying bias.

Official Title: Director of Intimidation
Real Title: Gang Member
Actual Job: Paints Buildings

Official Title: Auto Parts Dispersal Technician
Real Title: Car thief
Actual Job: Steals Cars

Official Title: Asset Re-Allocator
Real Title: Welfare Recipient
Actual Job: Watches Soap Operas

So, this whole concept of job titles is fluid. Titles now have to change as quickly as employees get wise to the scam, which, as I figure it, will probably be about every two weeks or so. Accordingly, as consumers, we will have to continue to use our old noggins as we try to figure out what any given person really does. I wish I had more time to explore this topic further, but I promised my Executive Supervisor of Domestic Technology that I would take out the garbage before I hurry off to an appointment with my Executive V.P. of Cranial Follicle Reduction, because I can't keep someone that important waiting.

More evidence that life is not fair

If life were fair, nobody would get sick...
or we would all get sick.

●●●●●●●●●●●●●●●●●●●●

If life were fair, everyone would have
the same parents.

●●●●●●●●●●●●●●●●●●●●

If life were fair, the phone wouldn't always
ring just as you get your pants down.

Could it be that some-times life is just not fair?

"Never use both feet to test the
depth of a stream."

- Heimlich Farfignugen

In the world of sports, life is not fair

For the one or two of you reading this book who may
not readily agree, here's proof.

Situation #1
Two minutes left in the game. My team is down 86
to 12. I am the only sub who hasn't played yet. No
fair.

Situation #2

Two minutes left in the game. The game is tied 48 to 48. I am a seldom-used sub. The coach tries to send me in. No fair.

See, for the athletically challenged, life is not fair

Time was if you were an athletically disadvantaged ball player who wanted to play on the same teams as the bullies, you would go out back and practice throwing rocks at the neighbor's barn. You couldn't use YOUR barn because your dad would kill you, but that's not the point. All great old time ball players: Honus Wagner, Babe Ruth, Ty Cobb, Robert Redford, and Kevin Costner became the greatest using this technique. As you threw these rocks day after day, you would fight through your fatigue and discouragement wondering how throwing rocks is supposed to help you since your game is golf.

Especially now days, doubting would probably indicate good judgement because, today it takes much more than just nervous barnyard animals to be a good enough athlete to be able to drive a Mazeratti 230 miles per hour through suburban neighborhoods while on crack, beat up your live-in girlfriend, and shoot friends and neighbors. Today's star athlete must have a sound understanding of nutrition, resistance training, performance enhancing drugs, deviant psychology, the criminal justice system, and crass self-promotion.

When I was a lad, chucking rocks worked, too, because society in general and coaches in particular didn't care whether or not a kid could play. In fact, they actually preferred lousy players. They only things they were worried about were character, class, and guts. They sent scouts out all over the country scouting around trying to find rotten players who had character so they could mold them into the kind of team who could win the championship by beating a well-coached, talented team made up of mean kids with mean parents, when all they had was a sense of humor and a charismatic coach. This happened all the time in those days. Most of my un-athletic friends played in the big leagues. Just ask them.

Today, life is less fair

Unfortunately, today's successful athlete must have much more than character and guts. He or she must have an attitude, tunes, and some "homies." He must have jewelry, furs and an agent, and above all, he must have parents who wear blue tights and capes and fly through the air hunting down criminals bent on destroying the world.

Today's potential athlete must know so much more about weight training, steroids, amphetamines, and nutrition. Now days if little Suzi is to have a chance to make the junior high team, she must begin lifting weights at around age two. Those with high school potential usually begin much earlier, otherwise the steroids Mom's injecting will build up toxins in her body such as lactic acid, Kaopectate, lanolin, and hard marshmallows from Lucky Charms. These could cause female fetal testicular cancer before the little super star will ever have a chance to get rich throwing games for gamblers in college.

The parent's responsibility

Yes, the role of the parent in kids' sports has changed. In the old days, all the parent of an athlete had to do was sit around in the stands and brag to other proud parents about her son's or daughter's accomplishments and point out that the official lacked a legitimate father.

Today, it is much more complicated than that. A budding athlete's parent must research to find the right super competitive junior league teams, buy airplanes for the team's travel comfort, or come up with another effective bribe to assure playing time, find creative ways to be seen every time the coach looks up from what he's doing, and come up with legitimate sounding excuses for holding the kid back in school for nine years so that he or she is older than some of the coaches.

Sounds exhausting, and it is. Sounds stressful and it is. Sounds like a bunch of crazy, zany, competitive, neurotic parental fun, and it is. And the truth is, if you're a super sports parent, you thrive in this element; you are the superstar in the bantam football game of life, and you have figured out that your child's success in sports has much more to do with your parental manipulation than it does your kid's character or ability.

What about kids with dopey parents?

If you happen to be a kid who likes sports, but who had the misfortune of being born to parents who aren't fiercely competitive and determined to live their lives through you, and who have screwed-up ethics and priorities, for you, life is not fair. You must find a way to enjoy sports and fend for yourself.

Sadly, as you've no doubt already figured out, being a good player isn't the answer because if you are good, all the super dad-coaches will perceive you as a threat to their kid, and through a sophisticated strategy of playing you at strange times, benching you for following their instructions, and messing with your stroke or shot, they will have you doubting you could successfully compete against poultry.

While you might think otherwise, sadly, being born with mediocre talent won't help you much either, since then the super-dad who coaches your team will have a legitimate excuse for playing you at weird times or not at all.

Fortunately, you DO have some great options, which we would like to share with you here. Unfortunately, we don't know what those good options are; therefore, we offer these:

Options for kids with parents incapable of taking care of them, athletically speaking

First, we recommend the band. It may surprise some of you, but bands compete too and they get to go to cool away games and play in sweaty uniforms. However, if that still doesn't satisfy your craving for competition, a second option which has been tried successfully for generations is to hang around the parking lot after games and beat up kids from the other schools, who's dads couldn't get them onto teams either.

If you are the type of kid who likes how your face looks now, a third viable option is to start playing some third world sport that none of the rich, or better-connected super dads are familiar with. This way, even if you have no money or are a complete dork, you can still be the expert because everybody else will have to depend on you for an explanation of the rules. You have absolute power whenever the other kids' parents have no idea what's going on. Heck, play Jai Alai, field hockey, or soccer, and they won't even know when to cheer. Better yet, have your dorky dad make up your own special sport and you can change the rules anytime you want to and keep the other super dads guessing.

I guess that if none of these work, there are always video games,...or, of course, you can always revert to throwing rocks at the neighbor's barn.

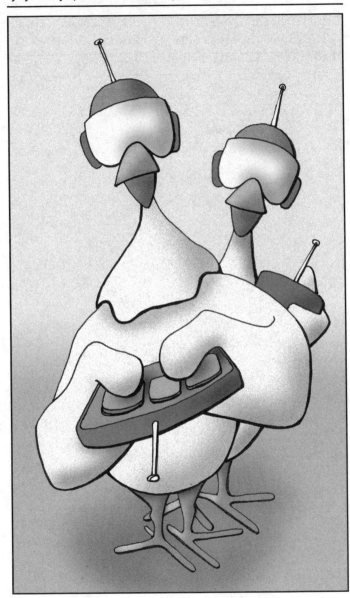

 100 years
from now life
probably still
won't be fair

"A rolling weasel probably got pushed
off the truck."

- Adenoid Stephenson

For your chagrin and enjoyment,
here are some absolutely failsafe
predictions about life in the
year 2103

In the year 2103, cell phone company ads will
lead you to believe that THEY will now be
paying YOU to use their services. Somehow,
however, your bill will still be three hundred
dollars-a-month.

Even though there will be 250,000 satellite channels, there will still be nothing good on.

● ● ● ● ● ● ● ● ● ● ● ● ● ● ● ● ● ●

The same 20 college football teams will still get all the money, TV time and national championships. The other 265 teams will be fighting for an at large birth in the Preparation H Zucchini Bowl.

● ● ● ● ● ● ● ● ● ● ● ● ● ● ● ● ● ●

After a plethora of successful lawsuits by animal rights advocates, all the evil burger manufacturers will finally be sent to jail. Most of us will be forced to buy our Big Macs and Kentucky Fried Chicken on the black market.

● ● ● ● ● ● ● ● ● ● ● ● ● ● ● ● ● ●

Congress will agree to a 3% election year tax cut, which somehow will result in a net increase to you of around 20%. Taxes are now 252% of your gross income. As a rider to the bill, Congress will get a pay raise.

● ● ● ● ● ● ● ● ● ● ● ● ● ● ● ● ● ●

Michael Jordan will be attempting his sixty-third comeback.

● ● ● ● ● ● ● ● ● ● ● ● ● ● ● ● ● ●

The Democratically controlled Congress will tie up some final loose ends on sweeping social legislation. They will now declare America safe from everything. In the bill, they will outlaw all potential causes of death: swimming pools, illness, poverty, poison, cancer, big business, old age, murder, car accidents, plane crashes, bears, jealous rages, crossing the street, chocolate, individual responsibility, French fries, farm accidents and embarrassment.

•••••••••••••••••

All the dams in the country will be emptied to protect the environment, but all the salmon, snail darters, and spotted owls will be dead anyway; eaten by starving people.

•••••••••••••••••

Allens will land in Amsterdam and nobody will notice.

•••••••••••••••••

Arab leader, No-sir, Arafat will lead a worldwide celebration marking the complete extermination of the Nation of Israel, the last two Israelis having been killed by a suicide car bomb just last week. Arafat will join the one surviving Egyptian and the two remaining Saudis praising the 1.2 billion suicide bombers who sold their souls to destroy the 850,000 Palestinian Jews.

99

Arafat will announce that now the job is done, he is moving to Monaco, quote: "Who would want to ever live in that godforsaken place?"

●●●●●●●●●●●●●●●●●●

Thanks to a few generations of stressful video games, human adolescent males will have begun to evolve exceptionally large, powerful thumbs.

●●●●●●●●●●●●●●●●●●

The Supreme Court will suspend all death sentences. Hence forth, the only capitol offenses will be smoking in non-smoking areas, racial profiling, and developing real estate in wetlands.

●●●●●●●●●●●●●●●●●●

Hollywood and the Internet will announce a long awaited multi-billion dollar merger. Hollywood spokespersons claim the merger will streamline entertainment. Hollywood will no longer have to waste time with peripheral filler like plots, stories, and news. They can now offer straight sex. Responding to alarmed critics, spokespersons will reassure the public noting that they will still retain some violence.

●●●●●●●●●●●●●●●●●●

Biff Steinbrenner, great grandson to George Steinbrenner, will pay $70 trillion to lure outfielder, Cynthia Bonds away from San

Francisco to play for the Yankees. Unfortunately, Cynthia's record setting 175 home run season will be cut short by a player strike. Both the players and the owners will claim they're losing money. Meanwhile, ticket prices will be raised to $80,000.00.

●●●●●●●●●●●●●●●●●●●

The U.S. Government and Lawyers will settle the largest ever class action suit compensating African Americans for slavery. African Americans will receive as compensation, "The South," while America will not be forced to admit guilt. As part of the same settlement, Native Americans will be given Manhattan as long as they return the beads and the twenty six dollars, The Irish will be given Chicago; The Chinese, the State of Washington; The Jews, Beverly Hills; The Mexicans, Texas; The Japanese, Hawaii; The Hawaiians, Japan; The Mormons, Missouri; The Cajuns, Nova Scotia; Women, the Social Security Trust Fund, Descendants of George Custer will receive the Titanic, Anyone unfairly voted out of Congress or formerly starring in a bad sit com which got the ax will receive the French Riviera and a pro-rata share of the interest on the national debt. The lawyers in the case will be given the Northern Hemisphere.

Order these additional Apricot Press Books

Humor Books

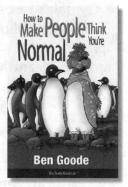

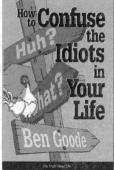

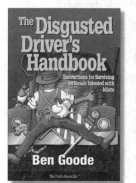

Order Online! www.apricotpress.com

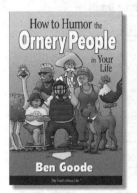

How to Humor the **Ornery People** in Your Life

Ben Goode

The Truth About Life™

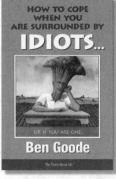

HOW TO COPE WHEN YOU ARE SURROUNDED BY **IDIOTS...**

OR IF YOU ARE ONE...

Ben Goode

The Truth About Life™

Whenever **Your Attitude Stinks...** Read This

Will be President for Food

"Another trendy book to make you feel OK when your life is a complete disaster"

Ben Goode

The Truth About Life™

Cook Books

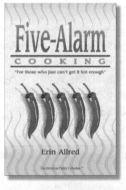

Five-Alarm C O O K I N G

"For those who just can't get it hot enough"

Erin Allred

The American Pantry Collection™

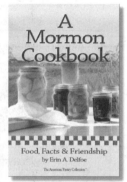

A **Mormon** Cookbook

Food, Facts & Friendship by Erin A. Delfoe

The American Pantry Collection™

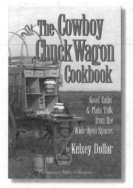

The **Cowboy Chuck Wagon** Cookbook

Good Eatin' & Plain Talk from the Wide Open Spaces

Kelsey Dollar

The American Pantry Collection™

The **All American**

Cookbook

The American Pantry Collection™

The **Chili &** **Tomato** Cookbook

The American Pantry Collection™

Apricot Press Order Form

Book Title	Quantity	x	Cost / Book	=	Total
_____	_____		_____		_____
_____	_____		_____		_____
_____	_____		_____		_____
_____	_____		_____		_____
_____	_____		_____		_____
_____	_____		_____		_____
_____	_____		_____		_____

All Humor Books are $6.95 US.   **All Cook Books are $9.95 US.**

Do not send Cash. Mail check or money order to:
Apricot Press   P.O. Box 1611
American Fork, Utah   84003
Telephone 801-756-0456
Allow 3 weeks for delivery.

Quantity discounts available.
Call us for more information.
9 a.m. - 5 p.m. MST

Sub Total = _____

Shipping = **$2.00**

Tax 8.5% = _____

Total Amount Enclosed = _____

Shipping Address

Name: _____

Street: _____

City: _____   State: _____

Zip Code: _____

Telephone: _____

Email: _____